First World War
and Army of Occupation
War Diary
France, Belgium and Germany

58 DIVISION
Divisional Troops
Divisional Trench Mortar Batteries
1 March 1917 - 28 December 1918

WO95/2995/6

The Naval & Military Press Ltd
www.nmarchive.com
Published in association with The National Archives

Published by

The Naval & Military Press Ltd

Unit 10 Ridgewood Industrial Park,
Uckfield, East Sussex,
TN22 5QE England
Tel: +44 (0) 1825 749494

www.naval-military-press.com
www.nmarchive.com

This diary has been reprinted in facsimile from the original. Any imperfections are inevitably reproduced and the quality may fall short of modern type and cartographic standards.

© **Crown Copyright**
Images reproduced by permission of The National Archives, London, England, 2015.

Contents

Document type	Place/Title	Date From	Date To
Heading	WO95/2995-5		
Heading	Trench Mortar Battys Mar 1917-Dec 1918		
War Diary	Field	01/03/1917	25/03/1917
Heading	War Diary Of 58th D.A. J.M.B. From 16/5/17 To 31/5/17		
War Diary	Field	16/05/1917	31/05/1917
War Diary	Field	16/05/1917	25/06/1917
Heading	War Diary 58th T.M.B. From 1st To 31st July 1917		
War Diary	In The Field	03/07/1917	30/07/1917
Heading	58th D.A.J.M. Brigade War Diary For August 1917		
War Diary	In The Sheet 57c 1/40,000 P.33a 3.3.	01/08/1917	31/08/1917
Heading	War Diary Of 58th D.A.J.M. Bs. September 1917		
War Diary	Sheet 27 D 22c Herzeele	03/09/1917	29/09/1917
Heading	War Diary Of The 58th Divisional French Mortar Batteries For October 1917.		
War Diary	Sheet 28 A 22d 8.5	02/10/1917	11/10/1917
War Diary	Sheet 28 A 28d72	13/10/1917	28/10/1917
War Diary	War Diary 58th (London) D.A.C.-Month Ending. 31/10/17.	31/10/1917	31/10/1917
Heading	War Diary Of The 58th Divisional Trench Mortar Batteries For The Month Of November 1917		
War Diary	Sheet 28 A 28 D 7.2	01/11/1917	30/11/1917
Heading	58th Divisional Trench Mortar Batteries. War Diary For December 1917		
War Diary	Longvillers	01/12/1917	12/12/1917
War Diary	Sheet 28 B 15c. 4.7.	12/12/1917	22/12/1917
War Diary	Sheet 28 B 28 Central	23/12/1917	30/12/1917
Heading	War Diary Of The 58th Divisional Trench Mortar Batteries January 1918		
War Diary	Sheet 28 B 28 Central Troistours	03/01/1918	20/01/1918
War Diary	Sheet 28 A 22d 7.2	20/01/1918	30/01/1918
Heading	58th Divl Trench Mortar Batteries War Diary For February 1918		
War Diary	Chauny	05/02/1918	24/02/1918
Heading	58th Divisional Trench Mortar Batteries War Diary For The Month Of March 1918		
War Diary	Chauny	01/03/1918	25/03/1918
War Diary	Blerancourt	26/03/1918	30/03/1918
Heading	58th Divisional Artillery Trench Mortar Batteries. April 1918		
Heading	War Diary Of The 58th Divl Arty Trench Mortar Batteries For April 1918		
War Diary	Audignicourt Le Mesnil	01/04/1918	30/04/1918
Heading	58th Divisional Trench Mortar Batteries R.A. War Diary For The Month Of May 1918		
War Diary	Francieres	01/05/1918	15/05/1918
War Diary	U24d 4.3 Sheet 57 D	16/05/1918	21/05/1918
War Diary	Warloy	22/05/1918	31/05/1918
Heading	58th Divisional Trench Mortar Batteries R.A. War Diary For The Month Of June 1918		

War Diary	Warloy U24d 4.3.	01/06/1918	18/06/1918
War Diary	Longpre	18/06/1918	19/06/1918
War Diary	Warloy	20/06/1918	30/06/1918
Heading	58th Div Arty Trench Mortar Batteries War Diary For July 1918		
War Diary	Warloy	01/07/1918	21/07/1918
War Diary	D4c 2.4.	22/07/1918	31/07/1918
Heading	58th Divisional Trench Mortar Officer. August 1918.		
Heading	58th Divisional Trench Mortar Batteries War Diary For August 1918		
War Diary		01/08/1918	15/08/1918
War Diary	Pont Noyelles	19/08/1918	27/08/1918
Heading	War Diary Of The 58th Divl F.M. Bs R.A. For The Month Of September 1918		
War Diary	Heilly	03/09/1918	04/09/1918
War Diary	B14d 7.2	06/09/1918	12/09/1918
War Diary	E7c 22	13/09/1918	28/09/1918
Heading	War Diary Of The 58th Divisional Trench Mortar Batteries R.A. For The Month Of October 1918		
War Diary	Lieramont	03/10/1918	03/10/1918
War Diary	E7c 22	06/10/1918	12/10/1918
War Diary	Hersin	13/10/1918	16/10/1918
War Diary	Bully Grenay	17/10/1918	18/10/1918
War Diary	O23b 4.7	19/10/1918	19/10/1918
War Diary	Lannay	22/10/1918	22/10/1918
Heading	58th Div Arty Trench Mortar Batteries War Diary For The Month Of November 1918		
War Diary	Lannay	03/11/1918	03/11/1918
War Diary	Rongy	04/11/1918	11/11/1918
War Diary	Grandglise G6c	12/11/1918	20/11/1918
War Diary	Grandglise Sheet 45 G6c	10/12/1918	28/12/1918

WO 95/2995/5

58TH DIVISION

TRENCH MORTAR BATTYS.
MAR 1917-DEC 1918

Box 2995

Trench Mortar Batterys

WAR DIARY
or
INTELLIGENCE SUMMARY.
(Erase heading not required.)

Army Form C. 2118.

Instructions regarding War Diaries and Intelligence Summaries are contained in F. S. Regs., Part II. and the Staff Manual respectively. Title pages will be prepared in manuscript.

Place	Date	Hour	Summary of Events and Information	Remarks and references to Appendices
Berles	March 1918 1st		All Batteries of the III Army T.M. School.	G.W.O.
	2nd		V/58, Z/58, & Y/58 T.M. Btns. move on motor T.M. Batteries march to GROSVILLE. X/58 and one section of V/58 Battery march to BERLES-AU-BOIS.	G.W.O.
	3rd		Taking over stores and equipment from 49th Division T.M. Batteries.	G.W.O.
	4th		Took over from 49th Division in the line. Carried out scheme between 5-0 & 9-0 P.M. 21 rounds fired on the OSIERBED and enemy trench in front of RANSART by V/58 & Z/58 T.M. Batteries. 14 rounds fired by V/58 T.M. B. on the TALUS and the BLOCKHOUSE. Rowli calibrating.	
	5th		8 rounds fired at enemy strong point by V/58 Battery. Rowli calibrating. Every available man from Medium Batteries employed in improving emplacements and clearing ammunition, both of which were found to be in a very neglected state.	G.W.O.
	6th		Work continued on emplacements and ammunition.	G.W.O.
	7th		Work continued on emplacements and ammunition.	G.W.O.
	8th		4 rounds fired by V/58 T.M. Battery at enemy strong point. 4 rounds fired by V/58 Battery at Sap Z.9.a. a shipment of infantry Rowli of both shots satisfactory. Sap Z.9.a. destroyed. Medium Batteries continued work on emplacements and ammunition.	G.W.O.

T.J.131. Wt. W708-776. 500000. 4/15. Sir J. C. & S.

WAR DIARY
INTELLIGENCE SUMMARY.
(Erase heading not required.)

Army Form C. 2118.

Place	Date	Hour	Summary of Events and Information	Remarks and references to Appendices
Field		6⁰⁰	14 rounds fired by Y/58 TM Battery on Sap M Z.9.a. as assistance to Z/58 Battery. Result satisfactory.	wnd
		9⁰⁰	20 rounds fired by Z/58 Battery at enemy wire opposite CAVENDISH Sap. Result satisfactory. Enemy retaliation caused of his first 2 rounds. 5 rounds retaliation fired by X/58 Battery at enemy front line north of MONCHY. Result satisfactory. 16 rounds fired by Y/58 Battery in support of patrol sent out to examine Sap Z.9.a. Result satisfactory. Work continued on emplacement and ammunition.	wnd
		10⁰⁰	42 rounds fired by Z/58 TM Battery at enemy wire opposite CAVENDISH Sap. A large number of duds are partly to faulty bits and partly to new striker cap. It was found that the number of duds could be reduced by tying on striker cap before firing. 90 rounds fired by Y/58 TM Battery at enemy wire north of FICHEUX. Result satisfactory and lanes cut 20 yards wide. Emplacements and leads in better order in this sector and consequently results of shooting more satisfactory. Y/58 TM Battery registered on BLOCKHOUSE with satisfactory results.	wnd
		11⁰⁰	4 rounds fired by Z/58 TM Battery at wire opposite CAVENDISH Sap. Result satisfactory as the new striker caps were tried on. 61 rounds fire by Y/58 Battery	

WAR DIARY
INTELLIGENCE SUMMARY.

Army Form C. 2118.

Place	Date	Hour	Summary of Events and Information	Remarks and references to Appendices
Field	11th Sept		At enemy wire north of FICHEUX and on the RANSART salient. Result very satisfactory north of FICHEUX but less satisfactory owing to faulty fuses opposite RANSART salient. 20 rounds fired by X/58 T.M. Battery at enemy wire north of MONCHY salient. Result satisfactory. Bone cut about 6 yards wide. R.E. quick and fatigue party worked during night on the but and emplacements opposite RANSART salient. Other emplacements also improved.	Wind.
	12th		45 rounds fired by X/58 T.M. Battery at enemy wire opposite CAVENDISH cop. Result satisfactory. Bone nearly 30 yards wide cut. 16 rounds fired by Y/58 Battery at enemy wire north of FICHEUX. Bone 20 yards wide maintained. 35 rounds fired by X/58 Battery at enemy wire north of MONCHY. Bone cut about 8 yards wide. Enemy had repaired this wire during previous night. 10 rounds fired by Y/58 Battery at wire opposite RANSART. Both emplacements badly damaged by enemy shell fire, and by thaw. R.E. party again worked during night to repair these emplacements. Y/58 T.M. Battery registered on LES TROIS MAISONS. Result satisfactory. Great difficulty experienced in supplying Heavy Ammunition to the emplacements owing to the condition of the ground and the thaw. Wind.	
	13th		29 rounds fired by X/58 T.M. Battery at wire opposite CAVENDISH cop. Result very satisfactory	

WAR DIARY
INTELLIGENCE SUMMARY.
(Erase heading not required.)

Army Form C. 2118.

Place	Date	Hour	Summary of Events and Information	Remarks and references to Appendices
Zulla	13th contd.		Enemy wire cut. 65 rounds fired by Y/58 Battery at enemy wire north of FICHEUX. Lane 30 yards wide cut. 45 rounds fired by X/58 Battery at wire north of MONCHY. Lane about 20 yards wide. 30 rounds fired by Y/58 Battery at wire opposite RANSART.	wd.
	14th		40 rounds fired by Y/58 Battery at enemy wire opposite RANSART. Lane cut 30 yards wide. Gun put out of action by enemy shelling and a bit destroyed. The good behaviour of Gunners Finch & Davis reported to both C.R.A. 40 rounds fired by X/58 TM Battery at wire north of MONCHY. Lane cut 20 yards wide. 30 rounds fired by Y/58 Battery at wire north of FICHEUX. Lane maintained 30 yards wide. 30 rounds fired by Z/58 Battery at wire opposite CAVENDISH Sap. Lane maintained 40 yards wide. 14 rounds fired in	wd.
× 15th			retaliation by Y/58 Battery. Ronville observed salifaying. × 160 rounds fired by the Hulluin Battery to improve gaps in wire Ronville salifaying. 14 rounds fired by Y/58 Battery in retaliation.	wd.
	16th		Hulluin emp enumerated. 5 rounds fired in registration by Y/58 Battery	wd.
	17th		124 rounds fired by Medium Batteries to improve gaps Ronville salifaying.	wd.
	18th		Enemy evacuate the trenches.	wd.
	19th		Mortars dismantled and concentrated at GROSVILLE and BERLES.	wd.
	20th		Ammunition collected, Mortars cleaned. Two Medium Mortars sent to I.O.M.	wd.

Army Form C. 2118.

WAR DIARY
INTELLIGENCE SUMMARY.
(Erase heading not required.)

Instructions regarding War Diaries and Intelligence Summaries are contained in F. S. Regs., Part II. and the Staff Manual respectively. Title pages will be prepared in manuscript.

Place	Date	Hour	Summary of Events and Information	Remarks and references to Appendices
Field	21st		Brigade concentrated at BERLES.	w.d.
	22		Fatigue party 25 men to assist D.A.C.	w.d.
	23		Fatigue party 50 men to assist D.A.C. at Adinfer. Brigade moved to GAUDIEMPRE	w.d.
	24		Stores, equipment &c. Batteries concentrated at GAUDIEMPRE	w.d.
	25		D.A.C. began collecting ammunition left in F. Sector	w.d.

W. Strother
C.W.R. T.H.O.
25/3/17.

Vol 3

CONFIDENTIAL
****
WAR DIARY
OF
58th DAC A.B.
From 16/5/17
To 31/5/17

Army Form C. 2118.

WAR DIARY of 58th D.A. Trench Mortar Batteries
INTELLIGENCE SUMMARY.
(Erase heading not required.)

Instructions regarding War Diaries and Intelligence Summaries are contained in F. S. Regs., Part II. and the Staff Manual respectively. Title pages will be prepared in manuscript.

Place	Date	Hour	Summary of Events and Information	Remarks and references to Appendices
Field	1917			
	16 May		Two 2" Trench Mortars taken over from 7' Division in BULLECOURT Sector reference ECOUST-ST-MEIN Edition 3 1/10000 M 28 a 2.2 by 1st detachment X/58 T.M.Bty	
	18	6am	X Battery detachment relieved in line by 2nd detachment of X Battery	
	18	9am	O.C. Y/58 T.M.Bty proceeded to V Army T.M. School taking one 2" Trench Mortars of Y/58 Bty with him	
	19		1st destroying of 12mm from V Bty reported to CRUCIFIX CORNER dump BEHAGNIES for duty	
	20	6am	X Bty detachment relieved in line by 3rd detachment of X Bty	
	"	9am	2 medium T Mortars ready for action in new positions at M 27 c 7.8.	
	22	6am	X Bty detachment relieved in line by 1st detachment of Z T.B.	
	24	"	Z " " " " 2nd "	
	25	"	Z " " " " 3rd "	
	26	—	Instruction in Anti-gas methods by Instructors attached to 58 D.A.C.	
	27	midnight	Z Bty detachment relieved in line by 1st detachment of Z Bty	
	29	"	Z " " " " 1st " of X Bty	
	31	2am	X Bty detachment withdrawn from line. Strong	

31-5-1917.

O.B. Warne
O.L.16 Captain R.F.A
58 D.A.

58

Copy

Army Form C. 2118.

Instructions regarding War Diaries and Intelligence Summaries are contained in F.S. Regs., Part II. and the Staff Manual respectively. Title pages will be prepared in manuscript.

WAR DIARY of 58th D.A. J 1600s
INTELLIGENCE SUMMARY. Vol I
(Erase heading not required.)

Place	Date	Hour	Summary of Events and Information	Remarks and references to Appendices
Field	1917 16 May		Two 2" Trench Mortars taken over from 7th Division in BULLECOURT. Map reference ECOUST–ST–MEIN Edition 3 10,000. U.28.a.2.2. by 1st detachment X/51st T.M. B'y	
	18th	6am	X Battery detachment relieved in line by 2nd detachment of X Battery	
	19th		O.C. V/51st T.M. B'y proceeded to V.B'y T.M. School taking one 2" Trench Mortar of Y/51st B'y with him.	
	"		V/Behagnies & 12mm from V.B'y reported to CRUCIFIX CORNER dumps	
	"		BEHAGNIES for duty	
	20th	6am	X B'y detachment relieved in line by 3rd detachment of X B'y	
	"	9am	2 medium T. Mortars ready for action in new position at U.27.b.9.8.	
	22nd	6am	X B'y detachment relieved in line by 1st detachment of Z B'y	
	24th	"	Z " " " " 2nd " "	
	25th	mid night	Z " " " " 3rd " "	
	26th	-	Instruction in Rifle-grenadthrowing by Instructors attached to 58th D.A.C.	
	27th & 28th night		Z D/B'y detachment relieved in line by 1st detachment of Z B'y	
	29th		Z " " " " 1st " "	
	31st	2am	X B'y detachment withdrawn from line. Barrow	

31st May 1917

W.R.M...
Capt. 51st RFA T.M.
Lt. M/O 58th DA

T.2131. W.t. W708–776. 500000. 4/15. Sir J. C. & S.

Army Form C. 2118.

WAR DIARY of 58th Div Hy Trench Mortar Batteries

INTELLIGENCE SUMMARY for June 1917.

(Erase heading not required.)

Instructions regarding War Diaries and Intelligence Summaries are contained in F. S. Regs., Part II. and the Staff Manual respectively. Title pages will be prepared in manuscript.

Place	Date	Hour	Summary of Events and Information	Remarks and references to Appendices
Field	1st		Camps moved from 10 (Sear 57) 20,000) B 28 a 8.8. Lieut Jones & 1 N.C.O. gunner sent to Headquarters of Corps & Army Artillery at ACHIET-LE-GRAND for collection of ammunition in backward areas.	
	2nd		D.T.M.O. & X/58th L.T.M. Bty proceeded to BULLECOURT to centralise 2" Mortars and ammunition. 2—2 mortars & 25 rounds of ammn at U 27 c 8.8. 6 Colt or MEIN 10,000 rounds. 1 L.t.C.O. & 20 men detailed for work at Divisional Bombing dump MORY.	
	3rd			
	4th		10 Officers 4 N.C.O.s & 20 men sent to 290" Brigade for work on positions — 3 telephonists sent to ammunition dumps — 3 Officers & 24 other ranks proceeded on courses to 5th Army Trench Mortar School VALHEUREUX	
	5th		2 Officers & 11 other ranks sent out collecting shell cases. 12 gunners sent to MORY dump.	
	6th		Capt. Tillney, O.C. V/58 J.M. Bty selected position for 1 Heavy Mortar at BULLECOURT U 26 c 7.6. 100 rds of 9.45" ammn sent to Mary lane. 1 Gun taken up to gun position. Gun pit being constructed.	
	7th		100 rds ammn taken up to Gun position of V/Bty. Lieut Gudgeon of Y/58 reported to BULLECOURT & rated position for 2" Mortar.	
	8th		Capt Tillney O.C. V/Bty killed by shell & 2 men wounded by debris. Lt Brown Capt Tillney buried in MORY cemetery.	
	9th		2 men of V/Bty killed, 2 men wounded. Lieut Gudgeon took over V/Bty.	
	10th		Lieut Bolam of Y/Bty went into action at BULLECOURT. New position for V/Bty selected by Lieut Gudgeon at U 21 c 2.3. New position for V/Bty selected from 2 Mortars position (ranging).	
	11		V/Bty fired 5 rounds.	
	12		Y/Bty fired 10 rounds. 2/Lieut Eden posted to V/58 L.T.M. Bty temporarily.	

Army Form C. 2118.

WAR DIARY
or
INTELLIGENCE SUMMARY.
(Erase heading not required.)

June 1917

Place	Date	Hour	Summary of Events and Information	Remarks and references to Appendices
Bullecourt	13	5am	Y Bty relieved in line by T/58 & 116 Bty. 40 rounds fired by Z Bty.	
	14		V/58 Stokes ready to fire. Emplact & dug-out completed.	
	16		20 rounds fired by Z Bty, last shot premature, but required remaking, blown in, reassembling.	
	17	5am	2" Mortar trench by enemy shell fire, dug-out destroyed, 2nd detachment of Z Bty relieved by 1st detachment.	
			Lieut J.C. Ball posted to 58" D.A. in Y/58.	
	19		No Ball proceeded to VALHEREUX on course of 2" Mortar.	
			New position in BULLECOURT for 2" Mortar in course of preparation.	
	23	10am	4 Stokes Trench Mortars & Mtrs Complete (in line) handed over to the D.T.M.O. T. Duncan.	
	24	noon	2 – 2" mortars (in line) handed over to the D.T.M.O. T. Duncan and 2 mortars received in exchange.	
			Camps moved to A 29. a 5 7.	
	25	4pm	2 Officers 3 N.C.O. & 38 other ranks sent to TRAMWAY DUMP, MORY for duty relieving 58th D.A.C.	

W.R.Turner
Captain R.F.A.
D.T.M.O. 58th D.A.

30 June 1917. D.T.M.O. 58th D.A.

Army Form C. 2118.

WAR DIARY
or
INTELLIGENCE SUMMARY.
(Erase heading not required)

Vol 3

Confidential

War Diary

58th T.M. Bty.

from 1st to 31st July 1917

Army Form C. 2118.

WAR DIARY
or
INTELLIGENCE SUMMARY.
(Erase heading not required.)

July 1917

Instructions regarding War Diaries and Intelligence Summaries are contained in F. S. Regs., Part II. and the Staff Manual respectively. Title pages will be prepared in manuscript.

Place	Date	Hour	Summary of Events and Information	Remarks and references to Appendices
In the field	July 1917			
	3rd		Orders received preparing to move	
	4th		X Y Z & V Batteries & D.T.M.O moved by Motor Lorries with 72.2" Mortars & Stores to FRICOURT CAMP B LINES. V/58 ammunition from French Battery.	
	5th		1 Corpl 2 Bomber & 27 other ranks sent to O.C. 58 D.A.C. for fatigues	
	6th	2pm	Inspection of Batteries by B.G.R.A 58 D.A.	
	7th		3 Officers & 60 other ranks to 58 D.M.S. for fatigues	
			1 N.C.O & 10 men to Town Mayor FRICOURT for fatigue	
	9th		3 Officers & 60 other ranks to 58 D.M.S. for fatigues	
			1 N.C.O & 10 men to Town Mayor FRICOURT for fatigues	
	10th		2nd Lieut W Eclaw posted to B/290 Bde RFA from V/58 T.M.By. 2nd Lieut R M Ruston posted from C/291st Bde RFA to V/58 T.M.B.By.	
	11th		D.T.M.O & V/58 T.M. By moved by Motor Lorry to Sheet 57 1/40,000 P 33 a 3.3.	
	13th		V/58 outfitted 1 Officer & 20 Other ranks & 11 Ammunition dumps NEUVILLE	
	14th		D.T.M.O & 2 Officers reconnoitred Right Sector front with a view to relieving portable trenches for trench Mortars X, Y, & Z Battery arrived from COMMECOURT 1 Officer & 30 Other ranks displaced to work at A.T.P. NEUVILLE until further notice	

WAR DIARY
or
INTELLIGENCE SUMMARY.
(Erase heading not required.)

Army Form C. 2118.

Place	Date	Hour	Summary of Events and Information	Remarks and references to Appendices
In the field	July 16th		2nd Lieut (Temp Lieut) R E Grogan, appointed Acting Captain whilst commanding a Heavy Trench Mortar Battery with effect from 9-6-1917	
	17th		2nd Lieut I D Williams, appointed Acting Lieutenant whilst commanding a section of RFA 5min division for battery with effect from 9-6-1917. 2 men sent to RFA 5min division for Artillery. 1 Officer & 30 other ranks sent to Divisional Headquarters 290th Brigade R.F.A. for the purpose of constructing dummy gun positions until further orders.	
	20th		1 N.C.O & 12 men sent to 58th Div for artillery further orders	
			1 N.C.O. 12 men to advance H.Q 291st Brigade R.F.A. for making gun positions until further orders	
	21st		1 N.C.O & 10 men to ARP NEUVILLE	
	22nd		1 N.C.O & 12 men relief to 291st Div advanced H.Q	
	23rd		1 - 9.45 Heavy Trench Mortar received in duty weather, may well stop moving & mortar telegram sent also moving.	
	24th		1 Officer & 25 other ranks sent to FOUR WIND FARM P.31 a.0.8. for enemy aeroplane shelling in shell holes.	
			1 N.C.O & 6 men sent to ARP NEUVILLE until further orders	
	27th		1 Officer & 20 other ranks to report daily to FOUR WIND FARM.	

WAR DIARY
INTELLIGENCE SUMMARY.
(Erase heading not required.)

Army Form C. 2118.

Place	Date	Hour	Summary of Events and Information	Remarks and references to Appendices
Suthfield	July 27	8.15	Relief party of 3 N.C.O's & 17 men despatched to 291st Bde R.F.A. advanced Headquarters.	
	30	8 a.m	Relief party of 1 N.C.O & 12 men despatched to 291st Brigade R.F.A advanced Headquarters.	

A.R.Munro
Captain R.F.A.
O.I.C.O 58th D.A.

D.T.M.O.
58TH
DIVL. ARTILLERY.
July
31-7-17

Army Form C. 2118.

WAR DIARY
or
INTELLIGENCE SUMMARY.
(Erase heading not required.)

58ᵗʰ D.I.T.M. Brigade

War Diary

— for —

August 1917

Vol 4

D.T.M.O.,
58TH
DIVL. ARTILLERY.

WAR DIARY
or
INTELLIGENCE SUMMARY.
(Erase heading not required.)

Army Form C. 2118.

August 1917.

Place	Date	Hour	Summary of Events and Information	Remarks and references to Appendices
Infte Sheet 51c 1/40,000 P.33a.3.3	August 1st		N.C.O.s from attached to 290th Brigade R.F.A returned to Camp. 9th Division arrived to take over.	
	2nd		N.C.O.s at NEUVILLE dump returned to camp.	
	3rd		V/58th Heavy Morters handed over to V/9th T.M.B'y. 12 tents handed over to D.T.M.O. 9th division. X & V/58th moved by Motor Lorries to 51B T2 & 7.6 and attached to 50th division. (HENIN) Y & Z/58th moved by Motor Lorries to Sheet 51c. T20 d.4.#1 and attached to 21st division. (ST LEGER)	
	4th	8pm	2 Officers & 7 N.C.O.s & 42 men carrying 2" bombs trench mortars to positions of V/50; X/50; Y/50 & Z/50.	
	5th		X/58th supplied 1 N.C.O. & 4 men to Z/50th for 3 days work. V/58th supplied 4 N.C.O.'s 25 men to V/50 carrying timber & tarpaulin covers for 9.45" Mortars. Y & Z supplied 1 Officer 5 N.C.O.s 10 - 2 inch M.Bs.	
	6th		ditto	
	7th		V/58th ditto	
	8th		V/58th ditto	
	9th		V/58th found 30 rations X/58th 100th officer & mortars of 21st H.C.B. at Sheet 51B 3W V/58th supplied tar party supplied on the 5th Aug at all ditto from the to pavilion on to the German front line.	

WAR DIARY
INTELLIGENCE SUMMARY
(Erase heading not required.)

Army Form C. 2118.

Place	Date	Hour	Summary of Events and Information	Remarks and references to Appendices
	10th	9 pm	3 N.C.Os 25 Gunners from V/58" to V/50" position	
	11th		Issued L.H. Rush detailed by VI Corps to assist V/2nd I No.B.Y. V/58" – L. Mortar positions flooded, unable to fire. Considerable firing near positions. V/5T" assisting V/50" at position ― for 3 days. X/58" ― Z/50" ― ― ― V/5T" position, enemy firing very considerable especially in vicinity of KNUCKLE AVENUE during morning. Fired 8 rounds from L.M. on to front line silencing German snipers. Fired 15 rounds on to front line opposite BEAUMONS LOOP, at positions to be machine gun emplacements, several direct hits on positions observed.	
	12th		2/58 supplied fatigues for V/58". V/58" 3 N.C.Os 25 men for V/50".	
	13th		V/58" fired 19 rounds on German front line opposite BEAUMONS LOOP. 1 N.C.O. 4 men from X/58" assisting Z/50 for 3 days. V/58" fired 19 rounds opposite BEAUMONS LOOP. V/5T 3 N.C.Os 25 men for V/50". 1 man of Z/58 wounded.	
	14th		Lieut. F. Desborough of V/58" posted to R.F.C. Headquarters for duty as Observer — posted strength of V/50". V/58"	

Army Form C. 2118.

WAR DIARY
INTELLIGENCE SUMMARY.
(Erase heading not required.)

Instructions regarding War Diaries and Intelligence Summaries are contained in F.S. Regs., Part II and the Staff Manual respectively. Title pages will be prepared in manuscript.

Place	Date	Hour	Summary of Events and Information	Remarks and references to Appendices
	15"		1 round of V/58" slightly wounded by shrapnel at WANCOURT. V/58" 3 & O.P 25 mm for V/50" pozdant	
	16"		Y/58" carried out registration on enemy front line. Rounds fired X/58" " " " ditto " " for V/50" 7 - "- V/58" 3 & 60. & 25 mm for V/50" X/58" 1 & 60. & " " for Z/50" for 3days	
	17"		V/58" 3 & 60. & 25 mm for V/50 Y/58" 1 portion of trench completely blown in & 30 bombers buried. 2nd position blown in every 1st premature caused by dust billets or pieces of shrapnel hitting bomb immediately before firing, our premature of a 10" round commenced wire cutting. 71 rounds fired.	
	18"	4-30am 10am 12-30pm	Enemy shelling by long range gun of V/58" & X/58" tents, one tent & canvas entry damaged, 2 Officers kennels hit also damaged.	
			Y/58" fired 9 rounds at hostile gun position, silencing enemy. V/58" 3 & 60. & 25 mm to V/50"	
	19"		V/58" ditto	
	20"		V/58" ditto X/58" 1 & 60. & 4mm for Z/50" Y/58" relieved in line	

A5834 Wt. W4973/M687 750,000 8/16 D. D. & L. Ltd. Forms/C.2118/13.

WAR DIARY
for
INTELLIGENCE SUMMARY.
(Erase heading not required.)

Army Form C. 2118.

Place	Date	Hour	Summary of Events and Information	Remarks and references to Appendices
	Aug 21st		V/58th men back from line	
			Z/58th — " —	
	22nd		V.X.Y.Z/58 moved by D.A.C transport to new area for billeting purposes Headquarters @ J.H.6.	Three hundred H.60 from V/58 sent to new area for billeting purposes
	23rd		1 N.C.O & 20 men supplied to B Echelon 58th D.H.6. for fatigue	
	24th		ditto	
	25		Orders received to prepare to move by rail.	
	26		Officers V/58 & Batteries to entrain their Horses etc. O.C. Z/58 returned to duty from leave	
	27		Entrained at ARRAS Station	
	28	9.30 am	Arrived at Camp 52 HOOGGRAAF map reference BELGIUM Sheet 28 G 26 c 7.9	
	29			
	30	2 pm	Moved to "Trench warfare" camp near DICKEBUSCH Map reference H 26 a 2	
	31st			

W. Morris
Captain R.F.A.
O.C. No. 58th D.A.

Army Form C. 2118.

WAR DIARY
or
INTELLIGENCE SUMMARY.
(Erase heading not required.)

War Diary
— of —
58gr D.A.I.C. 60s.

September 1917

D.T.M.O.
58TH
DIVL. ARTILLERY.

Army Form C. 2118.

WAR DIARY
INTELLIGENCE SUMMARY.
(Erase heading not required.)

September 1917

Place	Date	Hour	Summary of Events and Information	Remarks and references to Appendices
Sheet 27 D 22c HERZEELE	Sept 3rd	8 am	Moved from near DICKEBUSCH to HERZEELE Sheet 27 D 22c to billets at 79 80 81 & 82.	
	5"	9 am	V/58 Battery awaited lorries on road	
	6"	2 pm	Move to BROWNE HUT CAMP on the POPERINGHE - ELVERDINGHE Road Sheet 28 A 22 d 8 5.	
	8"	6 pm	D.T.M.O. attended Conference at R.A.H.Q.	
			Captn Gudgeon & 2nd Lieut Gilbey attended conference at advanced R.A.H.Q. (Canal Bank)	
	9"	9 am	V/58 T.M. B'ty proceeded to Camp of 48" T.M. B's for instruction in use of new 9"+5" Mark II M.L.T.M.	
		4 pm	Party of 2 Officers 3 N.C.O's & 57 men proceeded in lorries to "290" & "291" Brigade positions for fatigue - men not required	
		6 pm	1-6" Newton Mortar & Stores taken over from 23rd div. only 4 men required	
	10"	4 pm	ditto	
			B.T.M.O., Capt. Gudgeon & 2nd Lieut. Coates proceeded to ST JULIEN to reconnaître positions for T M's	
	11"	4 pm	Party of 2 Officers 3 N.C.O's & 57 men proceeded in lorries to Battery positions, 4 men only required.	
	12"		ditto	

Army Form C. 2118.

WAR DIARY
INTELLIGENCE SUMMARY.
(Erase heading not required.)

Instructions regarding War Diaries and Intelligence Summaries are contained in F. S. Regs., Part II. and the Staff Manual respectively. Title pages will be prepared in manuscript.

Place	Date	Hour	Summary of Events and Information	Remarks and references to Appendices
	Sept 12th	5pm	V/58th took over 1 Mor II 9.45" Mortar from 4th div at Sheet 28 H 2a 0595 & took it to ST JULIEN to position Sheet 28 c.12 c, transport from 5th DAC Party left in charge.	
	13th	8.30 am	1 Officer & 20 O.Rks ranks to SHELHOEK A.R.P. at A 23 B4.8 to fuze w.5 Ammunition	
	14"		ditto	
			V/58th - 9.45" Mortar ready for action Enemy shell set fire to Wood Shed a right of range opposite Morton position. Screen damage caused to Gun truks but no damage to gun itself.	
	15"		6" Newton Mortar dumped at the Cross roads ST. JULIEN Naval party for SHELHOEK A.R.P. fuzing ammunition	
	16"		SHELHOEK A.R.P. naval party	

WAR DIARY
INTELLIGENCE SUMMARY.
(Erase heading not required.)

Place	Date	Hour	Summary of Events and Information	Remarks and references to Appendices
	Sept 19th		V/58" fired 20 rounds at Hostile C.12 d.7.8. 5 effective hits. On the 7" round 8 of the enemy seen to leave the Hostile 5 dugouts over the ridge. 1 known brought in. 2 other targets, they thought to be nights of Cemetery and Sustained earthworks near JEWRY FARM, engaged and 5 rounds fired at each.	
	20"		V/58" - 2 targets engaged - 5 rounds only from every 10 light Mtrs fury towards at the 2nd target Ammunition and gun blown up by a shell apparently a 5.9". Gun lifted about 20 yards. No casualties, detachment under cover.	
	22nd		V/58" - working party to CHEDDAR VILLA.	
	23rd		X/58" rode over 6" Newton Mortar.	
	24"		V/58" - Marks III 9.45" Mortars taken up to ST. JULIEN forward.	

Army Form.C. 2118.

WAR DIARY
INTELLIGENCE SUMMARY
(Erase heading not required.)

Place	Date	Hour	Summary of Events and Information	Remarks and references to Appendices
	Sept 25		V/58 reconnaissance Morteros at D&c 65.55. 4 rounds fired at this target. 2nd round fairly effective. Firing Mode III q us Howitzer with Mode II charge. 10 rounds fired - CROSS COTTS (land). Howitzer right for range but weak for line. X/58 fired a 6" Newton Mortar into action at D7a 75.40. V/58 fired a 6" Newton Mortar into action at C.12 d 25.60 n.e. of Mebus at JURY FARM	
	26.		V/58 fired 4 rounds at 300 hour in direction of BOETLER. Heavy Machine gun fire in retaliation from CROSS COTTAGES & one mortar under firmament shell fire	
	27.	5-30 am	X/58 fired 28 rounds from D7a 75.40. Y/58 fired 8 rounds at strong point D7a d 95.25. rounds of shrapnel carried to cover mortars. Enemy aircraft Enemy shrapnel 2 rounds at extreme range	
	28.	1 pm	Inspection of T.M. Batteries by BG, RA. OC.	
		1-30 pm	V/58 party to ST. JULIEN to salve guns buried in by shell fire	
	29.	12 noon	Party of 20 other ranks to 291st Brigade R.F.A. for fatigue.	

W.S. [signature]
Captain Batt—
OC 160. 58 D.I.
30 Sept 1917.

A.5834. Wt. W4973 M68- 750,000 8/16 D. D. & L. Ltd. Forms/C.2118/13.

Army Form C. 2118.

WAR DIARY
INTELLIGENCE SUMMARY.
(Erase heading not required.)

War Diary
— of the —
58th Divisional Trench
Mortar Batteries
— for —
October 1917.

D.T.M.O.
58TH
DIVL. ARTILLERY.
31-10-17

Army Form C. 2118.

WAR DIARY
INTELLIGENCE SUMMARY.
(Erase heading not required.)

October 1917.

Place	Date	Hour	Summary of Events and Information	Remarks and references to Appendices
Sheet 28 A 22 d 8.5	1st		Ord	
	2nd	4pm	Camp moved from Sheet 28 A 22 d 8.5. to Sheet 28 A 28 a.7.2. upon the instructions of the area Commandant.	
	3rd		30 other ranks to LEFT GROUP at LA BELLE ALLIANCE for work with Batteries ditto 7 other ranks to CENTRE GROUP at HILLTOP 8 other ranks to RIGHT GROUP at WILSONS FARM 20 other ranks returned from digging 6 gun positions with 126" Bde A.F.A.	
	4th		6 men wounded and 1 man killed of men of above mentioned working party	
	6th		12 men for working party to CENTRE GROUP (D/82 position).	
	9th		Camp drained cleaned out & "funk" holes cleaned for Camp Commandant.	
	10th		20 X 60's gunners to Adjutant 291st Brigade R.F.A. for work at Battery positions digging gun pits.	
	11th		Captain Gudgeon R.E. O/C V/58 T.M. Battery awarded Military Cross Bomb: Wratten M.G. V/58 T.M. Battery awarded the Military Medal.	

Army Form C. 2118.

WAR DIARY
or
INTELLIGENCE SUMMARY.
(Erase heading not required.)

Instructions regarding War Diaries and Intelligence Summaries are contained in F. S. Regs., Part II. and the Staff Manual respectively. Title pages will be prepared in manuscript.

Place	Date	Hour	Summary of Events and Information	Remarks and references to Appendices
Sheet 28 A 28 d 7.2	13		5 N.C.O.s and 25 men to Adjutant 291st Brigade R.F.A to assist Batteries at gun positions	
	14		1 N.C.O & 4 men as relief for party working with 291st Brigade R.F.A	
	17		6 N.C.O.s and men to 290 Brigade R.F.A to report to R.S.M. the French.	
	19		Sergt Bayley E.J. 1/58th J.M. Battery awarded the Military Medal. Bomb. Wairston J. 1/58th J.M. Battery awarded the Military Medal.	
	23rd		N.C.O & 6 men as relief for a party working with 291st Brigade R.F.A	
	28		ditto	

A.B. Munro
Captain R.F.A.
O.I.M.O 58th D.A.

D.T.M.O.,
58TH
DIVL. ARTILLERY.
No.........
Date 31-10-17.

SECRET.   W A R   D I A R Y.

58th (LONDON) D. A. C. —   MONTH ENDING. 31/10/17.

PLACE.   DATE.   HOUR.   SUMMARY OF EVENTS AND INFORMATION.   REMARKS.

"NIL"

J. D. Lloyd Evans.
Lieut:Col.R.F.A.
Comdg. 58th (London) Divnl.Ammn.Column.

TO.
H.Q.R.A.
  58th (London) Division.
31/10/17.

58

Vol 1

War Diary

of the

58th Divisional Trench Mortar Batteries

for the month of November 1917

D.T.M.O.
58TH
DIVL. ARTILLERY.
No.
Date 30.11.17

13

Army Form C. 2118.

WAR DIARY
—of—
INTELLIGENCE SUMMARY. 58th Div. T.M. Bs.
November 1917.
(Erase heading not required.)

Instructions regarding War Diaries and Intelligence Summaries are contained in F.S. Regs., Part II. and the Staff Manual respectively. Title pages will be prepared in manuscript.

Place	Date	Hour	Summary of Events and Information	Remarks and references to Appendices
Sheet 28 A 28 a 7.2	Nov 1st	—	NCOs and men returned to Camp from attachment to 290th & 291st Brigades RFA	
	2nd	—	2 6" Stokes Mortars and one long Mark III 9.45" T.Ms and one Mark II T.M. with Mark III Barrage handed over to D.T.M.O. 7th Division	
	3rd	—	Move by lorries from A 28 a.7.2 to RUMINGHEM (RECQUES Artillery rest area)	
	4	—	Billets Nos 12-15-16-17-18-& 20.	
	7	—	290 RFA drew up arrangements to commence forthwith between D.T.M.O. and Brigade Commanders for the manning of T.M. Personnel on 18 pr. 8 & 5 Howitzer Runners	
	10	—	1 - 4.5 How taken over from D/290. Warning order to move Gun and Howitzer returned to Batteries.	
	11	—	1 - 18pr. from B/291st	
	12	—	V Z & X Batteries moved by lorries from RUMINGHEM to LONGFOSSE and bivied for night Y Battery unable to move owing to insufficient supply of lorries	
	13	—	V Z & X Batteries arrived at LONGVILLERS. 2 lorries sent back for Y/58 Battery (next rations)	
	15	—	Y/58 T.M. Battery arrived at LONGVILLERS.	

Army Form C. 2118.

WAR DIARY
or
INTELLIGENCE SUMMARY. November 1917.
(Erase heading not required.)

Place	Date	Hour	Summary of Events and Information	Remarks and references to Appendices
	16"		—	
	17"		2 - 18 pdr guns and 1 - 4.5" Howitzer and 3 Instructors received from 290 & 291st B.I.A. Brigades for instructional purposes	
	30"	10 a.m	Inspection of Batteries and Wheels by G.O.C., R.A.	

A.P.Hunter.
Captain, R.F.A.,
D.T.M.O. 58th Divn.

D.T.M.O.,
58TH
DIVL. ARTILLERY.
No.
Date 30-11-17.

58th Divisional Trench
Mortar Batteries

War Diary — for —

December 1917

Army Form C. 2118.

WAR DIARY
or
INTELLIGENCE SUMMARY.
(Erase heading not required.)

December 1917

Instructions regarding War Diaries and Intelligence Summaries are contained in F. S. Regs., Part II. and the Staff Manual respectively. Title pages will be prepared in manuscript.

Place	Date	Hour	Summary of Events and Information	Remarks and references to Appendices
LONGVILLERS	1917 Dec 3rd		Warning order received to prepare to move by road to II Corps area.	
			Two 18pr guns and one 4.5" Howitzer returned to 291st and 290th B'des R.H. respectively.	
	4th	9am	8 lorries reported. Move from LONGVILLERS to THIEMBRONNE area. Billets for night of 4/5 at FAQUEMBERGUE	
	5th	8am	Move off to ST MOMELIN. Billets for night 5/6 on ST. MOMELIN	
	6th	11am	Moved on to ZERMEZEELE area. Billets for night 6/7 at HARDIFORT	
	7th	8am	D.I.H.O & 2 Officers proceeded to T.M. demonstration at Second Army T.M. School	
			Move on to HAMOEK area. Billets at Camps Sheet 28 A 28 & 5 9	
	9th		Order received to move 10 Camps at Sheet 28 B 15 C & 7. (Sheldo Camps)	
	10th		Moved in Motor Lorries to new Camps.	
	11th		Work of Salvage of Guns taken over from D.I.H.O. 18th Division.	
	12th		2 Officers 5 N.C.Os & 35 men proceeded to billet at Canal Banks to commence work of Salvage.	

WAR DIARY or INTELLIGENCE SUMMARY

Army Form C. 2118.

December 1917.

(Erase heading not required.)

Place	Date	Hour	Summary of Events and Information	Remarks and references to Appendices
Sheet 28	Dec 12th		1 Sergeant & 6 men sent to 58th Reserve Gun School at B28 c.99.65 for duty.	
B15 c. & 7.	13		Two 6" Newton Mortars and two Long 9.45 Mortars taken over from 18th Division at B28 central (TROISTOURS)	
	14		Camp moved from B15 c. 4.7 to B28 central (TROISTOURS)	
	16		O.C. & 1 I.O. & Scout looked reconnoitred POELCAPELLE area reconnoitring district for possible Trench Mortar positions. V/58th T.M. Battery (made up to New establishment from Newton Batteries) proceeded to Toronto Army Trench Mortar School of Instruction on a course. 1 Officer & 7 other ranks proceeded to Second Army Trench Mortar School of Instruction	
	17		Two 6" Newton Mortars sent to DADOS 58th Division for transfer to 35th Division	
	22nd		Two 6" Newton Mortars taken over from 18th Division which had been taken away without corps sanction.	

Army Form C. 2118.

WAR DIARY
or
INTELLIGENCE SUMMARY.   December 1917.
(Erase heading not required.)

Instructions regarding War Diaries and Intelligence
Summaries are contained in F. S. Regs., Part II.
and the Staff Manual respectively. Title pages
will be prepared in manuscript.

Place	Date	Hour	Summary of Events and Information	Remarks and references to Appendices
Sheet 28	Dec 23rd		Guns for LICHFIELD A.R.P. in position each alternate night	
B 28 central	24th	6pm	Train of 4.5" Ammunition unloaded at LICHFIELD A.R.P.	
	30		G.O.C., R.A. inspected Camp and Mortars.	

D.T.M.O.
58TH
D.L. ARTILLERY.
31-12-17

S.H. Howe
Lieut R.F.A.
T.M.O. 58 Division

9 1519

War Diary

of the

58th Divisional French Mortar Batteries.

January 1918.

D.T.M.O.
58TH
DIVL. ARTILLERY.
January 31-1-18

Army Form C. 2118.

WAR DIARY
or
INTELLIGENCE SUMMARY.
(Erase heading not required.)

58 Divisional
Trench Mortar Batteries

Army Form C. 2118.

Place	Date 1918	Hour	Summary of Events and Information	Remarks and references to Appendices
Sheet 28 B 28 central	Jan 3rd		1st Push relieved Lieut Ball & working parties on Battery position	
TROIS TOURS	4		Lieut Dollar & party returned & Salvage of guns &	
	5		4 officers & 22 other ranks proceeded on Small Arms Tank Course of Instruction for course from 6th to 19 January 1918.	
	6		V/58 & X/58 Bty returned from Sheet 28 / No. 6 School proceeded at VAUX AMIENOIS and 1 officer and 3 other ranks returned from School	
	9		Army T.M. School at LEULINGHEM	
	12		D/1/58 D/2/58 35 Division in area POELCAPPELLE with a view to finding possible targets Hostile positions	
	14		Party returned from work at forward battery position give by Newton Mortars and lines (1.65 long) Mortars blown over	
	19		by 35 Divisional Battery 2 officers & 23 other ranks proceeded Small Army T.M. School at VAUX en AMIENOIS.	
	20		Corps moved from Sheet 28 B 28 central (TROIS TOURS) to Sheet 28 A 22 d 7.2 Bremois Camp	

WAR DIARY
INTELLIGENCE SUMMARY.
(Erase heading not required.)

January 1918

Army Form C. 2118.

Place	Date	Hour	Summary of Events and Information	Remarks and references to Appendices
Sheet 28 A22 d 7.2	20"		4 Officers & 22 Other ranks returned from Course at Second Army T.M. School	
	23"	12.30	Entrained at PROVEN en rte VILLERS-BRETONNEUX	
	24"	2 am	arrived at detraining station	
			Move to SAVY to HAMELET - 14cwt	
	28"	6am	X, Y, Z, Batteries move by lorry to CHAUNY - arrivd	
	29"	8am	V/58 Battery move by lorry to CHAUNY - arrivd	
	31"		Lieut Hamlett left for Fourth Army T.M. School for	
			Course of Instruction at the School	
	30"		2 Officers & 50 Other ranks detached for the 58" A.T.F.	

A.N. Howe
Captain RFA
O.C. 58" Div. Arty.

D.T.M.O.,
58TH
DIV. ARTILLERY.
Date 31-1-18

Vol 10

58th Div French Mortar
Batteries

War Diary

for

February 1918.

WAR DIARY or **INTELLIGENCE SUMMARY**

58th Div^l T.M. B^s

February 1918

Army Form C. 2118.

Place	Date	Hour	Summary of Events and Information	Remarks and references to Appendices
CHAUNY	Feb 5th		1 Officer & 20 O.Ranks arrived to take over 58th A.R.P. No 2 from 5th Army Brigade R.H.A.	
	6th		Order received from R.A.H.Q. for re-organization of T.M.B^s.	
	7th		X/58th and Z/58th T.M. B^{ty} personnel transferred to X/58 and Y/58 T.M. B^s to make these latter Batteries up to the new Establishment.	
	8th		Re-organization completed.	
	10th		6 Junior Officers received from D.A.D.O.S. 58th Div.	
	13th		O.C. 58th Officers reconnoitred Divisional front.	
	14th		ditto	
	18th		2/Lieut Johnson posted to 58th L.T.M.B^s from D.A.C. 1 Sergt, 1 Corpl & 3 Gunners surplus to new Establishment posted to V/VIII Corps Heavy T.M. Battery.	
	20th		Captⁿ Gudgeon R.E. and Batman posted to V/ Trier Army T.M.B.^s 6" M.L.T.M. received from D.A.D.O.S.	
	21st		12 Gas ejectors	
	22nd		7/D^l Wormos S.G. unposted to 58th D.A.C. 1/Lt R.M. Ruston posted to South Army T.M. School as Instructor.	

Army Form C. 2118.

WAR DIARY

58th Divl T M O Br

February 1918

INTELLIGENCE SUMMARY

(Erase heading not required.)

Instructions regarding War Diaries and Intelligence Summaries are contained in F.S. Regs., Part II. and the Staff Manual respectively. Title pages will be prepared in manuscript.

Place	Date	Hour	Summary of Events and Information	Remarks and references to Appendices
CHAUNY	Feb. 22		Lieut S.E. Yorke MC and Lieut J.O. Bollans promoted to rank of Captain whilst commanding a Medium T.M. Battery.	
	24		Personnel relieved by DAC Personnel at A.R.P.s 1 and 2	
			Work of getting T.M.B. Mortars into action commenced	

A.R Morris
Captain R.F.A.
D.T.M.O 58th D.A.

D.T.M.O.,
58TH
DIVL. ARTILLERY.
No. ....
Date 28-2-18

14 58th Divisional Trench Mortar S.A. 11
Batteries

War Diary

for the

month of March 1918.

58th Div Arty HQ.   **March 1918.**   Army Form C. 2118.

WAR DIARY
or
INTELLIGENCE SUMMARY.
(Erase heading not required.)

Instructions regarding War Diaries and Intelligence Summaries are contained in F. S. Regs., Part II. and the Staff Manual respectively. Title pages will be prepared in manuscript.

Place	Date	Hour	Summary of Events and Information	Remarks and references to Appendices
CHAMPY	1st		Lieut H. E. Young/Busty to be Bratsford posted to S.A.Bty from 291st Brigade RFA	
	4th		J.M. Conference at III Corps T.M.School BEAUMONT sur BEINE	
			Eight 2" M.L. Mortars returned to DADOS. 58th Divn upon exchange	
			from K.O.R.A	
	6th		J.M. emplacements in course of preparation at	
			Sheet 70 D NW H 15 d 38 40 2 mortars	
			Sheet 62 c SW T 29 b 30 85 2 "	
			" T 22 c 40 15 2 "	
			Sheet 70 D NW H 1 c 7 5 2 "	
			" B 27 c 3 4 2 "	
			" B 27 a 7 7 2 "	
			" B 27 a 5 5 2 "	
	10th		Alternative emplacements at "	
			4 wooden sub. seas for 6" Newton Mortar received from III Corps	
			workshops	
	11		Lieut C. E. Bratsford J an N.C.O. sent to 13" Corps at III Corps T.M. School.	
	12		160 rounds 6" F.M. Ammunition taken up to Right group trenches	

WAR DIARY
or
INTELLIGENCE SUMMARY.
(Erase heading not required.)

Army Form C. 2118.

Place	Date	Hour	Summary of Events and Information	Remarks and references to Appendices
CHAUNY	13th		170 rounds of 6" T.M. Ammn taken up to Left gun position. 60 rounds of 6" T.M. Ammn taken up to Right gun position.	
	18th		Instructions from BM 58th D.A. to have alternative positions to be able to shoot at the BUTTES de ROUY at 800 yards range. 3rd round of T.M. Ammn taken up to Right gun position. Positions reconnoitred at H.10.37.65 Sheet 70D N.W.	
	19th			
	21st		Positions subjected to heavy bombardment. 4 Mortars in Left Gun captured by enemy. Casualties saved. Captain A.D. Ockland 1 Wound. N.E. Young and 2 N.C.O.s missing.	
	22nd		2 mortars and beds at H.15.d.38.40 withdrawn to transport lines.	
	23rd		Situation normal on Right gun position front. Right guns subjected to fairly heavy shelling by 5.9" and gas shells. 2 positions in limbers nearly destroyed by enemy shell fire B.27.a. T.M. Headquarters moved from CHAUNY to OGNES and then to QUIERZY. 2 mortars of others W.P.Coltd have now been ordered from AMIGNY-ROUY.	
	24th		Move to BICHANCOURT and then to BOURGUIGNON	
	25th		Move to BLERANCOURT (3 g.s. Wagons on loan from Q.26)	

Army Form C. 2118.

WAR DIARY
INTELLIGENCE SUMMARY.
(Erase heading not required.)

Instructions regarding War Diaries and Intelligence Summaries are contained in F. S. Regs., Part II. and the Staff Manual respectively. Title pages will be prepared in manuscript.

Place	Date	Hour	Summary of Events and Information	Remarks and references to Appendices
BLERANCOURT	26"		Moved from BLERANCOURT to Att 4 Sec in positions withdrawn to BLERANCOURT.	
	25"		Over 200 rounds fired from Battery positions at request of Infantry Commander. Enemy	
	27"		Move from BLERANCOURT to AUDIGNICOURT ½ LE MESNIL. Enemy bombardment from 3 am till 6am	
	28"		D.T.M.O. carried out reconnaissance	
	29"		dlM	
	30"		12 Observers sent to assist in salving 2 guns of 6/291st Brigade RFA	

A B Munro
Captain RFA
D.T.M.O 58th D.A

D.T.M.O.,
58TH
DIVL ARTILLERY.
No.
Date 31-3-18

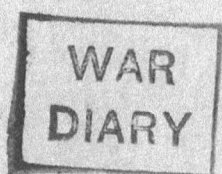

58th DIVISIONAL ARTILLERY TRENCH MORTAR BATTERIES.

A P R I L

1 9 1 8

Vol 12

War Diary
of the
5" Divl Arty Trench Mortar
Batteries
for April 1918.

D.T.M.O.
58TH
DIVL. ARTILLERY.
No.
Date

Army Form C. 2118.

WAR DIARY
or
INTELLIGENCE SUMMARY.

(Erase heading not required.)

April 1918.

Place	Date	Hour	Summary of Events and Information	Remarks and references to Appendices
AMDIGNICOURT LE MESNIL	1st	—	—	
	2nd	4 p	Left LE MESNIL and proceeded to CHEVILLECOURT	
	3rd	10 pm	Left CHEVILLECOURT proceeded to railhead at VILLERS-COTTERETS	
	4"	3 pm	Entrained at VILLERS-COTTERETS and LONGPONT	
	5"	9 am	Detrained at BACOUEL and LONGUEAU	
			Marches to BOUTERILLIE and CAGNY	
	6"		D.I.H.O conferences with 16" D.T.M.O.	
	7"		All Officers and personnel placed at disposal of CO 58" D.A.C. whilst not in action. 2 Batteries proceeded to GLISY leaving Guard for guns gunners at BOUTERILLIE	
	8"		H gas ejections & S tubes with howitzing guns drawn from DADOS 58" Dn	
	10"		D.I.H.O proceeded to 18" DA.S.Q at BOVES, receives instructions re possible position for 6" S.H. when ammunition supply available	
	11"		1 Officer & 14 other ranks awarded 39" D.T.M.O. to take up ammunition to position	
	12"		— ditto —	
	15"		D.I.H.O received instructions re defensive position	

A6945 Wt. W14422/M1160 350,000 12/16 D. D. & L. Forms/C./2118/14.

Army Form C. 2118.

WAR DIARY
or
INTELLIGENCE SUMMARY.
(Erase heading not required.)

April 1918

Instructions regarding War Diaries and Intelligence Summaries are contained in F. S. Regs., Part II. and the Staff Manual respectively. Title pages will be prepared in manuscript.

Place	Date	Hour	Summary of Events and Information	Remarks and references to Appendices
	16		D.I.&O's O.C. X & Y I.&O.Os carried out reconnaissance of Dum[p] field.	
	17"		All Officers and men withdrawn from dump work.	
	18"		4 mortars taken up to VILLERS BRETTONNEUX and put in action at O.35.c. 7.2. and O.35.c.6.4. (A lot of gas shell mixed with enemy fire)	
	19	9am	Guns ready for action	
		3pm	Guns withdrawn. Position full of gas.	
	20		D.I.&O. of 20" Division took over part of Line	
			2 mortars taken up to U T.18.b.88. (GENTELLES)	
	21"		160 rounds Ammunition taken up to T.18.b.88.	
	22"		2 mortars taken over from 61st D.I.&O. at U.16.c.88 and U.29.a.35	
			HANGARD 62 rounds fired from U.16.c.88 and U.29.a.35 Ammunition & emplacements taken over very wet.	
	23"		2 mortars handed over to 61st D.I.&O. in exchange for those taken over in the Line.	
			D.I.&O. submitted list of proposed emplacements near GENTELLES to C.R.A.	
	25"		2 Mortars moved from T.18.c.88 to T.18.a.0.3. Ammunition sheltered by using	

A6945 Wt. W11424/M1160 350,000 12/16 D.D.&L. Forms/C./2118/14.

WAR DIARY
or
INTELLIGENCE SUMMARY.
(Erase heading not required.)

April 1918.

Place	Date	Hour	Summary of Events and Information	Remarks and references to Appendices
	26		4 mortars received from D.T.M.O.S 58th Div to replace.	
	27		58th D.I. Group Order No 128 directed to withdraw from above all 6" Newton Mortars. Mortars withdrawn as directed.	
	28		Orders received from H.Q.R.A. to move at 10.40 am 29 April to a billetting area round CROUY — to ST PIERRE.	
	29		Proceeded by Route March to ST PIERRE via ST ACHEUL — AILLY — and PICQUIGNY.	
	30		Proceeded by Route March to FRENCHIERES via LONGPRÉ & COQUEREL. Billets in FRENCHIERES.	

A. Munro
Captain R.F.A.
D.T.M.O. 58th D.I.

D.T.M.O.,
58TH
DIVL. ARTILLERY.
No. ....
Date 30.4.1918

Vol 13

58th Divisional Trench
Mortar Batteries R A

War Diary

for the

month of May 1918

58th D.A.
I No. B3

Army Form C. 2118.

WAR DIARY
INTELLIGENCE SUMMARY.
(Erase heading not required.)

May 1918.

Place	Date	Hour	Summary of Events and Information	Remarks and references to Appendices
FRANCIERES	1st	—	In rest. Training Programme.	
	4th		Warning order from 16 O.R.S. — Prepare to move.	
	13th		News received that G.O.C. R.A Fourth Army would inspect Div. Artillery.	
	15th		D.T.M.O. proceeded to WARLOY with Brigade Major. 58th Div. Arty order No 131 to move received	
U24 d 4.3 Sheet 57D.	16		Move by Lorries to WARLOY-BAILLON — Billets in schools near Church.	
	17th		6 Guns and 5340 rounds 6" T.M. Ammunition taken over from D.T.M.O. 47".	
			Division. Portions of guns W20 c 85.40 – W20 d 25.55 – W20 c 80.70 – W20 c 65.80 W15 c 1.1. Emplacements under construction W20 c 70.40 and W15 c 10.13.	
	18th		6 guns handed over to D.T.M.O. 47" Div" in exchange for 6 taken over in line	
	19th		Shot carried out on Sunken roads & trenches in W15 b. Enemy garrison W20 c.	
	20th		Fired at junction of sunken road trench and track – W22 c 31 and trench in W22 c 9.3	
	21st		ditto W15 B 9.9 ditto W21 c. W27 c 5.6 V 24 c 3 d	
			D.T.M.O. reconnoitred for fresh positions (rear) – taken up in new positions & work on emplacements begun 4 mortars and 80 rounds complete of Ammunition	

Army Form C. 2118.

WAR DIARY
INTELLIGENCE SUMMARY
(Erase heading not required.)

May 1918

Place	Date	Hour	Summary of Events and Information	Remarks and references to Appendices
MARLOY	May 22nd		20 rounds fired at trenches in W21b. - W15d sunken road engaged	
	23rd		100 rounds of "Mustard" gas shells fell in & around BOUZINCOURT	
			2 mortars in V24c 5.3 ready to fire. Two small enemy dumps were reported at	
			Infantry to have been "put up" experts fire. Posts constructed at W11d & T.9.	
			Enemy fired about 200 rounds 77mm gas shells in the neighbourhood of V30a & V24c AND 1/24d 2.3	
	24th		Visual targets engaged and W27c & 9 near — W27d & 0.6 . 2 mm howitzers at W 1/24d 2.3 ready to fire	
	25th		21 rounds fired on special target by dividing field batty. Several direct hits	
			upon enemy trenches were observed. W27a own engaged	
	26th		O.J.M. O reconnoitred Brigade front with 17th Brigade staff	
			Bursts of fire m.m.g. were fired on Sunken road at W22 a 1.7 and W16 9.2 am	
			Quarry W27 c. 2.8 and trench W27 c 6.8.	
	27th		Bouzincourt heavily shelled by enemy. Fired on trenches at W27 d 1.5 from W22 a 1.7	
			About 100 rounds gas shell (mustard gas) at about W20.	
	28th		21 rounds fired at Orchard W2 d 3.5, trench crossing road W27 a 7.2	
			Trench junction W27c to 9 & trench 27c 3.9.	
			Enemy Artillery very active	

Army Form C. 2118.

WAR DIARY
INTELLIGENCE SUMMARY.
(Erase heading not required.)

May 1918

Place	Date	Hour	Summary of Events and Information	Remarks and references to Appendices
WARLOY	May 29	3 pm to 4 pm	In co-operation with the heavy howitzers observed fires at the following targets:-	
			Trench junction W.22.a.1.6 - Sunken road W.22.a.3.2 - Duckwalks W.22.a.4.4 - Sunken road W.22.a.5.8	
			Junction of trench & road W.27.a.7.2 - Ninety-pounder W.27.c.40.05 - trench W.27.c.30.90 - trench W.27.c.20.70 - Trig point W.27.c t. 10.10 & sunken road W.27.c.20.70	
			Enemy retaliated with a few rounds at W.15.c.3.1 and at W.20.d.9.2	
	30"		Shoots targets in W.27.b.9.4 and W.22.a engaged during the night	
	31"		Fired 20 rounds on sunken road & trenches in W.15 d & W.21.c. 5 rounds on trench junction W.21.c. and 10 rounds on Quarry W.27.c.	

A. R. Munro
Captain RFA
Commanding 58th Div Arty S.No.31.

D.T.M.O.
58TH
DIVL. ARTILLERY.
31st May 1918

58" Divisional Trench
Mortar Batteries R.I.

War Diary

for

the month of June 1918

Vol 14

WAR DIARY
INTELLIGENCE SUMMARY.
(Erase heading not required.)

58' D A T M Bs

June 1918

Army Form C. 2118.

Place	Date	Hour	Summary of Events and Information	Remarks and references to Appendices
WARLOY U.24.d.4.3.	1st			
	2nd		18" D.T.M. took over tactical command of Div Hy	
			D.T.M.O arranged with 18" D.T.M.O exchange of Battery position	
	3rd		18" D.T.M.O took over 6 Mortars + how at W20c2d, W15c, W14a.5	
			V.24.c.3.d. also 341 rds Ammunition	
	4th		58" D.T.M.O took over 4 reserve positions in HENENCOURT WOOD	
			V.26.d and 450 rds Ammunition	
	5th		10 Mortars taken over from 18" D.T.M.O in exchange for that handed	
			over at positions	
	7th		4 reserve positions at V.26.d. handed over to 18" D.T.M.O spares T.M.G	
	8th		Orders received to move on 9th June	
	9th		Mine frames & sand bags handed over to 47" I. Bs	
			Move by 5 lorries to LONGPRE near AMIENS	
	12"		D.T.M.O to IX French Corps Manoeuvres	
	13'		Training Programme	
	14th 18th		ditto	

Army Form C. 2118.

WAR DIARY
or
INTELLIGENCE SUMMARY.
(Erase heading not required.)

Instructions regarding War Diaries and Intelligence Summaries are contained in F. S. Regs., Part II. and the Staff Manual respectively. Title pages will be prepared in manuscript.

Place	Date	Hour	Summary of Events and Information	Remarks and references to Appendices
LONGPRE	18th		O.Y.b.O. proceeded to WARLOY to arrange relief with 47"D.T.M.O	
	19th	10pm	Orders to move received	
	20th	9am	Move from LONGPRE to WARLOY by 5 lorries	
WARLOY			6 - 6" mortars taken over in the line by X.55 T.M.By from 47" T.M.Bs at E.13a. 25.50	
	21st		E.7d E.13a & D.18d By headquarters at E.13a. 25.50. By no front line trench junctions / targets attacked with good effect	
	22nd		25 rds no ranger from Y.50th sent to assist B.291st Infantry D.T.M.O. reconnoitred & reported to H.Q R.A on suggested new positions for the defence of LAVIEVILLE. Over 100 rounds were fired on enemy trenches & strong point Cow By position shelled with 20 & 25 5.9s	
	23rd		2 shots carried out with 5 guns upon enemy trenches in E.8c E.13a & E.13d. By Cw gun were shelled by enemy from 3.15 to 30.15pm.	
	24th		90 rds fired on enemy trenches & at E.14d E.19d & E.14d. (6 guns firing) By to do shelled with 5.9s from 7.30am till 8.15am	

A6945 Wt. W14422/M1160 350,000 12/16 D.D. & L. Forms/C/2118/14.

Army Form C. 2118.

WAR DIARY
or
INTELLIGENCE SUMMARY
(Erase heading not required.)

Place	Date	Hour	Summary of Events and Information	Remarks and references to Appendices
WARLOY	June 25"		Reconnoitred for new positions in defence of LAVIEVILLE in case our dumps	
			120 odd fired on enemy front line from E14c E20a E14n E13d	
			and E19c. G.O.C. R.A. visited B'dy positions	
			Enemy shelled E7c with 15" to 4.2	
	26	6 p.m.	fired 30 odd on E14a 20.60 – E8a 35.90 and roads on T.M. position by	
			Brick woods at E14a 70.40 on retaliation – (at request of Infantry) enemy T.M.	
	27"	10.45 a.m.	About 25 gas shells fell on enemy	
		5 p.m.	50 rds fired in retaliation as enemy front line system widened	
		6 p.m.	E8c, 75.25 and 13d 60.00. Instructions to get on with revised positions recd.	
	28"		Enemy M.G at E13c 95.15 registered at the request of the Infantry	
			60 odd fired on enemy front line system	
	29"	4 p.m.	Hun attacked 29th Bde returned. Bus fires at hostile M.G. at E13c 95.10	
			40 odd fired on enemy trenches & roads at E14c 50.50 E13d 50.45 E8c 80.30 & E14c 20.05. Battery.	
	30"		Stores were carried out, 5 guns on the following targets – E9c 80.25 – E14a 80.90 E14a 25.70 E14c 15.05 E13a 90.25	
		9.35 p.m.	Co-operated with Artillery 9th Y° – 60 rds fired on E17d 30.30 – E13d 65.00	

A. B. Horner

Captain RFA

O/C 58th DA

D.T.M.O.
58TH
DIVL. ARTILLERY.
30-6-1918

58th Div. Arty Trench Mortar Batteries.

War Diary

for

July 1918

Vol 15

58 Div! No D.
RA

Army Form C. 2118.

WAR DIARY
or
INTELLIGENCE SUMMARY.
(Erase heading not required.)

July 1918.

Place	Date	Hour	Summary of Events and Information	Remarks and references to Appendices
WARLOY	July 1st	5.15 6.30 7.30 8.40 pm	Commenced new positions for defence of LAVIEVILLE. The following targets engaged. Junction of E14c 80.90 – Junction E14c 85.90, TM at E8c 80.25. Sap at E14a 80.90. Quarry at E14c 25.65. MG E14a 95.10. Cross roads E14c 15.05 MG E14c 60.05 and Cross roads E13d 90.25	
	2nd	5.30 p.m.	10 rds fired at TM E8c 20.90	
	3rd		Q.1.40 o succeeded as Cont. Captain. A.G. Rait. Acting Q.1.40	
		3.50m 6.50	HQ rds fired on hostile TMs Cross roads & Quarry	
	4th	3.10 pm	Co-operated with plane strive. 100 rds fired on hostile defences. TMs were so	
	5th	10.15 pm 3.10 6.10am	Retaliatory shoot on TMs – E13d E20a E14a carried out on request. Infantry 30 rds Bombardment for our raid carried out on defences – E13d E14c E14a E8d.	
		2.40 pm 9.20 pm	60 rds fired on TMs E14a E13d Quarry E14c in retaliation.	
	6th	1.15 am 10 pm	130 rds fired on hostile TMs Quarry. defences in E13d E14c E14a E13d and E19c.	
	7th	10.50 am 8.10 pm	10 rds fired on Quarry Crossroads MG J Trenches in E14c E13d and E19c. 60 rds fired in retaliation on TMs – E14a and E14c.	
	8th	2 pm	30 rds fired on Quarry in E14c 25.65 & Trench E19c 20.50	
	9th	6.30 pm	110 rds fired on TMs E14c & E20b and E13d	

WAR DIARY
or
INTELLIGENCE SUMMARY.
(Erase heading not required.)

Army Form C. 2118.

Place	Date 1918	Hour	Summary of Events and Information	Remarks and references to Appendices
	July 10	6 pm	59 rds fired on Groups C. Hostile T.Ms. derelict tanks & trenches in E14c.	
	11"	3.30	67 rds fired on Groups of hostile T.M. B.3 Down tanks & trenches E14c, E13 d &	
	12"	6pm	60 rds fired on Groups A.B.C.D Hostile T.Ms and enemy trenches in E14c	
	13"	3 pm	65 rds fired on enemy trenchmen E8c, E8d, E19c,d	
	14"	3 pm	65 rds fired on Target B. Tank trenches E13d E14c, E8c,d	
	15"	5 pm	70 rds fired on enemy trenches & earthworks E13d, E14c.	
	16	2.30p	130 rds fired on earthworks E13d. M.G. E14c. enemy T.Ms in E13d.	
	17"	7.30	100 rds fired on Groups I and G. T.Ms and wire in E13d	
	18"	11.30	80 rds fired on wire entries in E13d, E13 c and Groups B hostile T.Ms.	
	19"	3 pm	103 rds fired at several targets	
	20"	6.30	52 rds fired on Groups A and D and tank & trenches in E14c & E13d	
			4 Officers & 52 other ranks left for course of instruction at the Fourth	
			Army T.M. School MILLY FLEBEAUCOURT	
	21"	7 am	52 rds fired on Barton E14c Quarry E14c,d	
			H.Q.'s Headquarters moved up to Quarry in D 19c. 2.4	
	22nd	6 p.	115 rds fired on Groups A & B on Bank & trenches in E13d.	
Dec 24.				

Army Form C. 2118.

WAR DIARY or INTELLIGENCE SUMMARY.
(Erase heading not required.)

Instructions regarding War Diaries and Intelligence Summaries are contained in F.S. Regs., Part II. and the Staff Manual respectively. Title pages will be prepared in manuscript.

Place	Date 1918 July	Hour	Summary of Events and Information	Remarks and references to Appendices
Dec 24	23rd	3.30 pm	6 rds fired on Grpos A.B.&J hostile T.M's and suspected M.G. Ellrs.	
	24"	3.	9 rds fired on Grpos J and Bank and new E14c a. & E13 at	
	25"	6.15p	8 rds fired on Grpos Ram J. hostile T.M's and arranging in E14a & E19c	
		3pm	D1/160 of 5" Australian Divn called in taking over. 58" D.A. orders to 1.144.	
	26"	12 noon	D1/160 proceeded to HENLY on taking over.	
	27"	12.5p	fired on Quarry E14c & Grpos J and R T.M's	
	28"	11am	10 rds fired on Quarry E14c on request of Infantry	
	28"	9am	4brds fired on Grpos B' R' & J. harassing & in retaliation	
	29"	12.45pm	co-operation with 5" Australian Division - 16 rds fired on Quarry E14c and triangle of trenches in K1d and K2a as ordered by 58 D.A. Order No. 146	
	29"		11brds fired harassing & retaliatory fire on hostile T.M's E14c Quarry &c	ditto
	30"		To do hrs	ditto
	31"	12.5	58" D.A. order to 147 on relief of 58" Divl Arty by 25" Divl Arty received	

Arthur C. Ball
Captain R.G.A.
7D/160 58" D.A.

58th Divl. Artillery

58th DIVISIONAL TRENCH MORTAR OFFICER,

A U G U S T   1 9 1 8.

58th Divisional Trench
Mortar Batteries.

War Diary for

August 1918.

WAR DIARY
INTELLIGENCE SUMMARY

August 1918

Army Form C. 2118.

Place	Date Aug	Hour	Summary of Events and Information	Remarks and references to Appendices
	1st		D.T.M.O. 25" Div Arty took over 5 Mortars & Ammunition - forward position and 6 reserve positions (LAVIEVILLE) and Ammunition	
			H.Q. removed from Quarry in D.40.24 to 1 Main Street, WARLOY.	
	2nd		Took over 10 - 6" Mortars from 25" D.T.M.O. in charge for those handed over.	
	5th		Move by Lorry from WARLOY to Billets in PONT NOYELLES. O/D.T.M.O reconnoitres Durenslefont for possible T.M. position.	
	6th	1am	1 Cpl & 12 men report to B/291st Bde R.A. for fatigue & rations. setting wires at J.24.c.6.3	
	8th		11 other ranks to advanced H.Q.R.A. as working party for day.	
	10th		1 Officer & 35 other ranks to 290 Bde forward HQ as forward working party.	
	11		1 Officer & 12 other ranks to ABBEVILLE for remounts.	
			Capt Trengrove proceeded up the line to bring back German T.M. for the 406.	
	12th		14 other ranks to advanced H.Q.R.A. working party	
	15		1 Officer & 17 other ranks to A.R.P. Chipilly for duty.	

WAR DIARY
or
INTELLIGENCE SUMMARY.
(Erase heading not required.)

Army Form C. 2118.

Place	Date 1918 Aug	Hour	Summary of Events and Information	Remarks and references to Appendices
PONT-NOYELLES	19	—	D.T.M.O. 3rd Australian Division is taking over. Officers & other ranks returned from attachment to Batteries.	
	20		D.T.M.O. to forward R.I.T.O.P.	
	24		G.O.C., R.A. inspected detachment at gun drill	
	25		Move by lorry to HEILLY Sheet 62D J 20 12.	
	26		1 Officer & 20 other ranks to A.R.P. K 13 d to takeover from 50" DA 1 Officer & 20 other ranks to A.R.P. K 17 central ditto.	
	27		1 Officer to A.R.P. E 18 central.	

A R Horner
Captain RFA
D.T.M.O. 58th D.A.

D.T.M.O.,
58TH
DIVL. ARTILLERY.
No.
Date 31-8-1918

War Diary
of the
58th Divl. T.M. Bs. R.A.
for the
month of September 1918.

D.T.M.O.
58TH
DIVL. ARTILLERY.
30-9-1918

58 D.N. T.M.B.

WAR DIARY
INTELLIGENCE SUMMARY.
(Erase heading not required.)

September 1918 Army Form C. 2118.

Place	Date	Hour	Summary of Events and Information	Remarks and references to Appendices
HEILLY	3rd		2 6" Mortars sent to Workshops MONTIERES for fitting of new spades attachments	
	4		Instructions received from 58 D.R.A. for the selection of all German Light T.M's and Ammunition in the Divisional area	
B14d7.2.6"	6		Move from HEILLY to HAUT ALLAINES L4d.7.2	
	7		2 mortars fitted with spare attachments of Bordo T.M.G. moved forward to D.15.00 290° B.11 RFA HQ. to be in close communication	
			with 173rd Inf Bde	
	9		Orders re getting away many TM's into action as possible before midnight	
	10		2 mortars got into action at corner to common EPÉHY 30 rds fired	
	11		5.7 cm Light German Minenwerfer 282 rds Amm" stored in dug-	
	12	5/oo	Move to NURLU for night	
E7c22	13		Move to LIÉRAMONT E/c 22	
			2 additional 6" Mortars & 1 76cm German T.M. taken up & got into action at: 1 6" & 1 7.6cm E12a 40.40 = 1.76 mm	
			at E12a 50.42 and 1 6" motar at E12a 60.35	
			2 motars taken up at	

WAR DIARY
or
INTELLIGENCE SUMMARY.
(Erase heading not required.)

Army Form C. 2118.

Instructions regarding War Diaries and Intelligence Summaries are contained in F. S. Regs., Part II. and the Staff Manual respectively. Title pages will be prepared in manuscript.

Place	Date	Hour	Summary of Events and Information	Remarks and references to Appendices
	2/5/18 13		J. Sept. new action at W.29.d.2.2.	
	14	1.7.6am	T.M. taken up & got into action at E.12.a.57.42.	
	15"		90 rds fired between 10.45am and Dawn on Tulse road & Flo F7b F7a.	
	16"		28 rds fired at trans on stray farm W.30.d, W.30.c & F.6a & F.6c.	
	17"		120 rds fired between 2am & 5.30am on stray farm Flo Eber W.30.d W.30.c & a	
	18"		275 rds fired on stray farm between 8pm & 5.20am on stray farm — Jochia W.30.d.7.3. Wood farm Cropad road & stratus keep Meteren roads. 2 mistures & 1.7.6cm Mortars moved forward to westport 1/3 Inf. Brigade to X.25.c.3.8.	
	19"		Instructions received to reconnoitre O.M. Counts and the Dundee — Ravelsberg X.26.d.6.9 to X.27.a.0.0 to X.26.b.8.4 & thence N.E. van Trench Mortar position from which LIMERICK POST & Crown-Trenchan X.21.d & 22.c could be bombarded.	
	20"		Further instructions received re selection of T.M. positions to bombard LIMERICK POST and KILDARE POST and to provide protective barrage after capture of these posts by 173rd Inf. Brigade	

Army Form C. 2118.

WAR DIARY (cont)
INTELLIGENCE SUMMARY.
(Erase heading not required.)

Place	Date	Hour	Summary of Events and Information	Remarks and references to Appendices
	Sept 1918 23rd		58 DA order No. 173 issued withdrawal of Battery from position and concentration of Batteries at LIERAMONT to receive further orders.	
	25		58 Div Arty to come under orders of 906 Australian Corps.	
	28		Officers selected to take over 4" Australian A.R.T at E.14.6.85. – PERONNE to inspect for X Bty (4 Officers & 53 other ranks) proceeded to IV Army Junior Officers School at SAILLY FLIBEAUCOURT for "V course" assembling on the 29" inst. and dispersing on the 15" October 1918.	

A. M. ?????
Captain RFA
OJ/CO 58 DA

War Diary

of the

58th Divisional Trench Mortar Batteries R.A.

in the month of

October 1918.

WAR DIARY
or
INTELLIGENCE SUMMARY.
(Erase heading not required.)

Army Form C. 2118.

58th Divisional Trench Mortar Battery R.A.
October 1918.

Place	Date	Hour	Summary of Events and Information	Remarks and references to Appendices
LIERAMONT	3rd	0.0.	3 N.C.Os. to A/290 Brigade R.F.A. to assist	
E.7.c.2.2	6"		7 N.C.Os. & men to 291" Brigade to assist	
	11"	4p	Entrained at TINCOURT railhead	
	12"	4p	Detrained at HERSIN - billeted in HERSIN	
HERSIN	13"		1 Officer & 7 other ranks sent for duty at A.R.P. tube St PIERRE	
	15"		O.I.K.O. (Captain A.O.Ball) posted to 3rd Balloon Wing R.A.F. as Observer	
			Captain to immense M.G. into work duties of O.I.K.O.	
	16"		O.I.K.O. set over from O.I.K.O. 24 Divison - moved to BULLY GRENAY one & sub-sector	
BULLY GRENAY	17"		2 mobile trench Mortar carriages received from O.I.B.O.	
			returned	
	18"		Moved by lorries from Bully-Grenay to MONTIGNY sheet 41.sw O.23.b.4.7	
O.23.b.4.7	19"		Officers and disk ranks of X Battery returned from IV Army	
			Trench Mortar School at SAILLY FLIBEAUCOURT	
			Y Bty & 2 mobile Trench Mortars and Ammunition proceeded to	
			BACQUERY - keeping in touch with Infantry Brigade during advance	
LANNAY	22nd		X Bty moved from MONTIGNY to LANNAY	

Alfred O Ball
Captain
J.C. 58 D.A.
1/58 O D.T.M.B. 58 D.A.

Oct 3/19

58th Divl. Arty
Trench Mortar Batteries

War Diary

For the month of

November 1918

Army Form C. 2118.

58th Divl Trench Mortar Battens RA
WAR DIARY or INTELLIGENCE SUMMARY
(Erase heading not required.)

November 1918

Place	Date	Hour	Summary of Events and Information	Remarks and references to Appendices
LANNAY	Nov 3rd		O.C. T.M.O. carried out a reconnaissance of the Divisional front for possible Trench Mortar positions	
RONGY	4	0900	"X" B'y moved from LANNAY to RONGY. 200 rds T.M.G received	
	7		"Y" B'y returned from attachment to D.A.C. 4 Mortars and 120 rounds of Ammn taken up to position reconnoitred at BLEHARIES - Left Sector. Headquarters location D.25.c.65.65 Sheet 44 N.E. Mortars in action in gardens in rear of BHQ.	
	8		2 Mortars ready for action on Right Sector Divisional front. All mortars withdrawn from positions (on enemy retiring) and concentrated at RONGY when orders received from the O.R.A. and 90 rds T.M.G. Battries attached to Sectors of the D.A.C. 2 mobile mortars only taken & moved forward remainder of Mortars sub-becos beds & stores left at RONGY under guard, at billet 23 Rue du L'eglise.	
	10		Move with D.A.C. to WIERS. Location K.4.a.5.5.	
	11		Move from WIERS by road to GRANDGLISE, Sheet 45 G.6.c	

Army Form C. 2118.

WAR DIARY (cont.)
INTELLIGENCE SUMMARY
(Erase heading not required.)

November 1918

Place	Date	Hour	Summary of Events and Information	Remarks and references to Appendices
GRANDGLISE	12		7/DTMO awarded M.C.	
G 6 c			7/DTMO appointed Town Major GRANDGLISE	
	16		"X" Bty Officers attached for duty to 290 Bde R.F.A. and "Y" Bty Officers attached for duty to 291st Bde R.F.A.	
	20		6 Gunners transferred to 15" Dur. Trench Mortar Batteries.	

[Stamp: D.T.M.O., 58TH DIVL. ARTILLERY. No. ..... Date 30-11-18]

M Wedderall
Captain. M.C. R.G.A.
7/DTMO 58 DA.

Army Form C. 2118.

WAR DIARY
INTELLIGENCE SUMMARY.

(Erase heading not required.)

December 1918   58th Div. Arty F. to B.

Place	Date	Hour	Summary of Events and Information	Remarks and references to Appendices
GRANDGLISE Sheet 45 G6c	1918 Dec			
	10		Lieut J.N. Tarleton took over duties of Town Major, GRANDGLISE and from Capt. H. Bell M.C. evacuated to hospital	
	14		4 men (minus) sent to I Corps Concentration Camp for demobilization	
	17		1 man (minus) ditto	
	28		Lieut W.I. Hamlett took over duties of Town Major from Lieut J.N. Tarleton.	

M.I. Hamlett
Lieut R.F.A.
1/DTMO 58' DA

D.T.M.O.
58TH
DIV'L ARTILLERY.
Date 31-12-1918

www.ingramcontent.com/pod-product-compliance
Lightning Source LLC
Chambersburg PA
CBHW081444160426
43193CB00013B/2377